POWERS

ANARCHY

POWERS

ANARCHY

Created and Produced by

BRIAN
MICHAEL
BENDIS
&
MICHAEL
AVON
OEMING

Color Art: **PETER PENTAZIS**

Typography: **KEN BRUZENAK**

Editor: **K.C. McCRORY**

Collection Editor: **JENNIFER GRÜNWALD**

Book Design: **PATRICK McGRATH**

Cover Design: **TIM DANIEL**

Business Affairs: **ALISA BENDIS**

Previously:

Detectives Christian Walker and Deena Pilgrim work out of the special homicide unit in charge of cases that involve Powers.

Walker has been off the force for almost a year due to his scandalous interview with the press about the federal corruption in law enforcement.

POWERS VOL. 5: ANARCHY. Contains material originally published in magazine form as POWERS VOL. 1 #21-24. First printing 2015. ISBN# 978-0-7851-9307-4. Published by MARVEL WORLDWIDE, INC., a subsidiary of MARVEL ENTERTAINMENT, LLC. OFFICE OF PUBLICATION: 135 West 50th Street, New York, NY 10020. Copyright © 2003 and 2015 Jinxworld, Inc. All rights reserved. Powers, its logo design, and all characters featured in or on this issue and the distinctive names and likenesses thereof, and all related indicia are trademarks of Jinxworld, Inc. ICON and its logos are TM & © Marvel Characters, Inc. No similarity between any of the names, characters, persons, and/or institutions in this magazine with those of any living or dead person or institution is intended, and any such similarity that may exist is purely coincidental. **Printed in the U.S.A. Manufactured between 11/21/2014 and 12/28/2014 by R.R. DONNELLEY, INC., SALEM, VA, USA.**

10 9 8 7 6 5 4 3 2 1

Freezer=decapitated

3/4

Bug

4/1

Nickel and Dime "gunshot" 4/...

Socio "hanging" 4/20

FUCK ME IN THE EAR.

WHAT IS *THIS*?

SOME- BODY CUT OFF HIS HEAD.

NO WITNESSES TO *THIS*, EITHER.

WE DON'T KNOW *WHAT* HAPPENED, EXCEPT OMEGA 6 TIED HIM TO THE POLE HERE, FOR US, I GUESS, BUT...

NO WITNESSES? IT'S RIGHT IN THE MIDDLE OF...

THEY WERE ALL WATCHING OMEGA 6 BURN,

NOBODY EVEN NOTICED IT 'TIL WE GOTS HERE.

NOBODY NOTICED SOMEBODY LOPPING OFF HIS HEAD WITH ONE SLICE?

NOW, THAT'S A JADED FUCKING...

WAIT...

WHERE'S THE HEAD?

AAAGGHHH!!

MAN, THAT'S FUCKING INSANE!

OOF!

YEAH, DON'T STOP AND HELP HIM, YOU RETARDS!

SHE LOOK FAMILIAR TO ANY OF YOU?

NOPE

FUCK!

NOPE.

NO.

CAN WE RUN IT THROUGH THE COMPUTER?

I WAS JUST ASKING.

THIS ISN'T STAR TREK.

IT DOESN'T WORK THAT WAY- FUCK!

PUT THE CAMERA *DOWN*-- GOD!

THIS IS AWFUL!

MAN...

PEOPLE SUCK.

HEY!

THERE! STOP!

ZOOM IN,

HOW IT *DOES* WORK IS WE'LL RUN IT BY THE OTHER DEPARTMENTS-- THE FEDS...

AND END UP GOING TO THE MEDIA.

NOT NECESSARILY.

PLEASE.

NOT NECESSARILY

LISTEN, LISTEN, LISTEN...

WE DIDN'T DO ANYTHING. WE JUST DID A BACKGROUND CHECK ON HER,

WE WANTED TO TRY TO GET OUR FILLER PIECE READY WHEN YOU PICKED HER UP.

TRISH...

CREEEEEEEE

POLICE! FREEZE!!!

THE TIRES! JUST THE TIRES!!

I KNOW.

BAM!

I'M NOT GOING TO BE TALKING TO YOU.

BET YOU ARE.

I WANT TO TALK TO WALKER.

HE DOESN'T WORK HERE ANYMORE.

WALKER!

YEAH!

OH, MY GOD...

YEAH, YOU MISSED.

LET'S GO. COME ON...

COME ON...

OH, MAN...

I KNOW

DID YOU SEE THAT?

I DID.

WHAT?

YOU JUST TRIED TO ESCAPE...

EVERYONE, GET BACK!

OH, NO...

..WALKER..

THIS IS THE *POLICE*, FUCKFACE! PUT YOUR WEAPON *DOWN!!*

DEENA, STAY *THERE*! I *GOT* IT! DON'T *MOVE*!

WALKER!!

YEAH!

KAOTIC CHIC.

THE WORDS HAVE CREEPED INTO OUR PUBLIC CONSCIOUSNESS LIKE A VIRUS...

YET NO ONE IN THE CITY, NOT EVEN THE SUPERHEROES IT THREATENS, KNOWS FOR SURE WHAT IT MEANS.

FLIPSIDE
Hosted by COLLETTE McDANIEL

COLLETTE McDANIEL
Author of "Who Killed Retro Girl?"

COLLETTE McDANIEL
Author of "Who Killed Retro Girl?"

WORDS SPRAY PAINTED OVER THE CORPSE OF RETRO GIRL AS SHE DREW HER FINAL BREATH THAT FATEFUL DAY AT MORRISON ELEMENTARY SCHOOL.

HER KILLER, JON JACKSON STEVENS, TOOK THE MEANING OF THOSE CRYPTIC WORDS TO HIS GRAVE.

RETRO GIRL

JON JACKSON STEVENS

AND THEN THERE'S HARVEY GOODMAN.

AFTER THIS FOOTAGE WAS SHOT OF HER AND HER PARTNERS IN CRIME DESECRATING THE SITE OF OMEGA 6 VIOLENT PUBLIC BURNING...

... A HALF DOZEN MURDERS WERE PINNED ON HARVEY AND HER GROUP, NOW KNOWN AS "THE KAOTIC CHIC MURDERS."

HARVEY GOODMAN

BUG

WELL...

WELL, WELL...

WELL, I THINK WE SHOULD BE PARTNERS AGAIN.

WHAT DO YOU THINK?

WHAT- DO-YOU- THINK

I--HA-- I'VE BEEN WAITING FOR YOU TO JUST ONCE ASK ME WHAT I AM THINKING ABOUT SOMETHING

AND YOU FINALLY FUCKING DO...

...AND--AND ...I GOT NOTHING.

I'VE ASKED YOU BEFORE...

WANNA BET?

MAN, I--YOU WERE THE WORST PARTNER ON EARTH... EVER!

YOU KNOW THAT? I WAS GLAD TO BE RID OF YOU.

JUST A BIG, FUCKING, SELF-RIGHTEOUS DICKHEAD.

BUT THEN I THINK BACK...

...AND I THINK HOW WELL WE CLOSED ALL THOSE FUCKERS, AND HOW-- HOW--

(WELL OK, I'LL ADMIT SOMETHING TO YOU HERE)

WHEN I SAW THE CLIP OF YOU ON THAT DICKHEAD'S SHOW, AND YOU WERE TELLING EVERYONE ABOUT HOW YOU AND ZORA WERE--

--WERE CLOSER THAN YOU HAD LET ON.

..I--I CRIED MY EYES OUT, MAN.

I FELT SO BAD.

I REALLY-- I HURT FOR YOU.

AND I THOUGHT: HOW CAN I BE FEELING FOR THIS GUY WHO DOESN'T LET ME TALK...

...WHO DOESN'T TRUST ME...

(NOT EVEN ENOUGH TO TELL ME HE WAS GETTING MARRIED TO START WITH...)

FOR A GUY WHO FUCKING LOOKED ME IN THE EYE AND ACCUSED ME OF SOME SERIOUS SHIT--

--HOW CAN I CRY FOR YOU WHEN YOU'RE HURTING?

BUT THEN I THINK: I GOTTA CARE ABOUT YOU. I--I GOTTA.

WHAT'S THE ONLY OTHER ANSWER? NOTHING.

I CARE ABOUT YOU.

POWERS
COVER GALLERY

POWERS

22 | 2.95 CANADA
POWERS

KAOTIC CHIC

"POWERS IS A WORK DESERVING OF THE RARELY JUSTIFIABLE TITLE...
MASTERPIECE!" - GRADE: A!
-COMIC BUYER'S GUIDE

BRIAN MICHAEL BENDIS
MICHAEL AVON OEMING

"One of the best collaborations in comics today!"
-Ain't-it-cool-news

BRIAN MICHAEL BENDIS
MICHAEL AVON OEMING

OEMING INTERVIEWS BENDIS AND VICE VERSA

So, this is something you don't see everyday. The creative team of the comic you just read raking each other over the coals a bit. We always thought our private talks were more interesting than the interviews we gave, so here, exclusively for you, is an unedited discussion between Mike and myself on everything that we could think of at the time we thought to do this. We may make this a regular feature in the collections.

This section also features rough page layouts by Mike Oeming.

OEMING: Why writing? Why have you chosen writing over art? I know one comes more naturally to you than the other and you never had a commercial style, but clearly you could be drawing some of your own stories, if not on a monthly basis, as a special issue or so. I could clearly see you drawing an *Alias* issue.

BENDIS: Life is opportunities. I took the art gigs when they came, both in comics and outside of comics. And now it's the writing gigs that are coming. I just read a great quote: "A career is about what you say no to." That is so true. I think about what I have decided not to do and why and wipe my brow in relief, you know? I supported myself as a graphic artist for almost twelve years. I will draw again. I love to do it. Plus, I am so much more successful as a writer, it's almost sad.

OEMING: You started as an artist, doing work for local mags and papers, even doing caricatures—at what point did you want to start writing?

BENDIS: The first time I drew a caricature at someone's fucking nightmare *bar mitzvah*. That did pay well and it funded all my crime graphic novels, but it has to be the lowest form of artistic expression on the planet, I really hated it. And as I hated it more and more my caricatures got meaner and meaner.

What is the worst job you ever took for money? And don't say *Powers*, ass.

OEMING: It was last year. I did the cover to a children's book called *The Blue Avenger*. I thought it would be fun. Hey, this is a "real book" I'd be doing a cover to. It pays really well, too. But nothing on this earth is worse than a book editor. They know everything about words, but nothing about pictures. Example, they say they want a Zebra, so I give them a Zebra, but then they ask for no stripes. I say, then it will look like a horse...No, they say, they want a Zebra, just no stripes. So I do it...Then they say it doesn't look like a Zebra. This story had something to do with a donut. So I drew one in the background like they wanted. Well, I put sprinkles on it, because without sprinkles or something, it just looks like a tire. They say "make it glazed," so I do and it looks like a tire. I assure them with colors, it will look like it's glazed. Then they say it looks too literal, it should be a "cosmic donut." No shit. So I made it look like there was space swirling out of the fucking thing like it's giving birth to the universe. In the end, I don't think any of us were happy with it. This was worse than doing porn comics in the early '90s, because at least then I could get excited, jerk off, and get something out of it. But this was pure torture.

When did writing really click for you, meaning you went beyond writing stuff to facilitate your art to where the art was there to facilitate your writing?

BENDIS: It was never about writing only to facilitate my art. It was more about just overall storytelling. The only thing odd about the whole thing is how natural the expression of writing is for me and what a struggle

drawing is and was, and yet I wasn't even considering the idea of writing for a living, because that seemed just insane to me.

Why did you start drawing? Not when, why?

OEMING: I'd always drawn because of my mom. She would draw a lot. She had a drinking problem (well, actually drinking wasn't the problem, she did that fine, but the rest of her life went to shit) and I had to be raised by my Aunt and Uncle for about four to seven years. For the first five, she didn't live with us, she was trying to get sober, but still drinking. Anyway, she'd write me letters with drawings in them. I've always associated art with life, I guess, because of that. I remember once getting a letter from her with some happy clowns on it she drew. For the most part, I was patient, I knew what was wrong with her and it was just a waiting game until she got better. But when I got that letter, it set me off. Usually she drew flowers and butterflies, but this had happy clowns on it and I guess a happy clown was the last thing I felt like. I remember ripping it up. I was about five. The only thing worse than the happy clowns was ripping them apart. We kept drawing though, and it became a cheap pastime.

I stopped drawing shortly after mom came to live with us. I think I didn't "need" it anymore, but most importantly, I remember a teacher telling me a drawing I did wasn't very good and that I was much better than that. So I stopped. I didn't really draw for a long time after that. A few times, but not all the time like I had been. Then I moved from Jersey to Texas (mom and I did this once before when I was younger and she first got custody of me, but we came back to Jersey) in about the 6th grade and it was terrible for me. I didn't adjust at all. It was actually traumatic. I locked myself in my room, I learned to jerk off properly and read comics. Funny how those two go together so well. Anyway, I found comics at a flea market and fell in love with Spider-Man all over again. I started tracing and tracing. We moved back to Jersey, I went from tracing to copying to drawing. Then *X-Men Annual #9* came out and it was all over for me. Art Adams made me want to be a comic book artist for sure, and I've been on that path ever since.

Before Robert McKee's *Story*, what was your major writing influence? Was it simply reading other writers that turned you on, or was there a specific school of thought that you worked on? Or was it mostly instinctual?

BENDIS: I was taken away by three writers: Richard Price, David Mamet, and Woody Allen. The three best dialogue writers in the history of any medium. Characters that talk to each other and not at each other. I studied their work, and it sent me on a quest for the work they loved and I started reading that, and then I started making my own decisions as a writer. People hate when I say this, but I am totally self-taught, never took a class.

You write, as well. What are your influences other than *Penthouse Forum*?

OEMING: Well, not to kiss your ass because I've already got the *Powers* gig, but at this point it's you. Not so much what or how you write, but the things we discuss through the making of *Powers* have become the new tools I carry with me in writing and storytelling. There are writers and books you've introduced me to and ways to study a story that have equipped me with new writing skills. So you can only blame yourself when I'm off writing and not drawing *Powers*!

Before you, I was into superficial writing. I wrote stories around cool things, not around story. That was one problem with *Ship of Fools*. I gave Bryan Glass *ideas* to write around, a bunch of disjointed weird shit he had to try and put together in a story, so in the end it had no focus. We plan on reissuing *Ship of Fools* slightly rewritten and some art moved around to open up the story and give it focus. At that point, my main writing influences were Mike Baron from *Nexus*, which I feel is the best overall series ever written, and Douglas Adams of *Hitchhiker's Guide*. I still love that stuff.

BENDIS: Also, not many people know how many things you can do and how varied your art and linework can be. What got you on the road you are on now?

OEMING: Shortly before *Powers*, I think I had finally started on a good "realistic style." I did a short *Kabuki* story like that. But then at the same time, that's when my career hit a dead end (like a lot of pros in the mid-'90s crash) and I had to get a "real job." My son Ethan

was born so I needed to bring in money on a regular basis. So, with the new job and baby came less time to work, so I needed to focus on a more simple, less time-consuming drawing style. It had really started about a year earlier when I was really trying to be Alex Toth, but then I found Bruce Timm and married the two in a way that worked and was less time consuming. Don't think you can just jump into a simple style, it's actually very difficult at first stripping the work down like that. It really makes your weaknesses shine through, it takes a long time to develop. So I eased into it. I tried working on *Batman Adventures*, but I still couldn't do the style. I think I got real comfortable with it just as I started *Hammer of the Gods*. Then *Powers* happened, and by that time I was really into it. Look at the first trade of *Powers* and the work coming out now, you can still see a progression. While it's still there, I've gotten pretty far away from Timm and Toth, almost more into general animation, especially during the *Supergroup* and *Anarchy* story arcs, when I was using the mono dead lines. They look like animation cells.

Was there a genre you were into before crime stories?

BENDIS: Marvel superhero comics.

OEMING: At what point did those crime stories really take hold of you?

BENDIS: Yeah, this is still odd to me, because I didn't know that this is what I wanted as a writer until I started writing. Everything that came out of me were these poppy Jim Thompson graphic novels and I didn't even know who he was. No one was more surprised than me. It's the idea that in crime fiction you can examine a character by really throwing him into a corner and seeing what he will do.

OEMING: Do you think that interest in crime comics, the idea of someone being thrown into a corner emotionally, is a reflection of your own experiences? I know like many people, you didn't have a perfectly happy childhood. Do you think any residual anger from when you were younger is what attracted you to crime stories?

You really introduced me to crime stories and noir. Who introduced it to you, or did you discover it, consciously or subconsciously? I've always been into European Mythology, but it wasn't until recently that it became conscious. I can trace it back to my childhood. How far does a fascination with crime stories go back for you?

BENDIS: Hmm...I started my love of the genre in comic form. All those crime comics like Steranko's and all the Munoz novels, really got under my skin. Then, like my writer heroes, I backtracked to find Jim Thompson and Hammett. I read every Thompson novel in a three-week period, like I was taking a course in it.

Then I saw the *Visions of Light* documentary and they started talking about the rules of film noir. I knew them, but I had never heard them spoken out loud before, and when I heard them I literally stood up in the theatre and yelled, "Halleluiah," I knew that this was for me.

OEMING: When a story comes to you, what part of it comes first--the overall idea or specifics of the story?

BENDIS: Could be anything, sometimes it's just an image, like a dead superhero lying in a playground, or a one liner that you think is so good you start constructing a story about it for the soul purpose of publishing that one line.

When you read the script, what do you do, just read it through and take it in, or start thinking as the artist immediately? What goes on in that head of yours? We have never discussed that.

OEMING: I think I'm lucky, because images come to my head immediately. I really mean immediately, sometimes before I finish the sentence I know what the panel is going to be. I rarely even do a second layout or change a panel when I first draw it, unless it doesn't fit the story and you ask me to, which is fine. But images come to me like an attack, to the point that it's distracting. I think that comes from my childhood. My Aunt and Uncle always had the radio on--if the TV wasn't on, the radio was, and when we slept, we slept with the radio on. It was always easy listening, that '70s and '80s singer-songwriter stuff. Crosby, Stills, and Nash, James Taylor, Billy Joel, Cat Stevens, Carly Simon, Simon and Garfunkel, Gary Numan, Harry Chapin, that sort of stuff. All those songs had stories. So I'm sleeping there, or trying to sleep and listening to these songs. Each of them told a loose story and with my eyes closed, I saw the stories or played them out in my head. I'd have to say that singer-songwriters may have been the single most important writing influence on me; artistically as well, because that's where the immediate imagery comes from.

To this day I hear a song and I can build a story around it. That's where *Hammer of the Gods* came from, Led Zeppelin's "The Immigrant Song." *"We come from the lands of ice and snow, from the midnight sun and hot springs flow, the Hammer of the Gods will drive our ships to new lands, to fight the horde, sing and cry, 'Valhalla, I am coming!'"*

Those words made me write what became *Hammer of the Gods*, although it has little to do with the words of the song...well, except the last line, that's almost the plot!

Do you think in terms of the themes, then the story builds around that, or do you have an idea you bring the themes to?

BENDIS: After I decide on the story, I start questioning what the purpose of it is. I really don't think enough people do this—ask themselves why they are writing what they are writing. It needs to say something other than just being cool. And sometimes I clearly state the purpose in the material and other times I don't. I just let it hang there. And sometimes the theme can derail the original story and take it in another direction. You have to be open to it. You've seen me do that, do a 180° on what I told you the story was going to be, because the characters or theme dictate it.

OEMING: That's awesome. I try to do that, too. I either have the meaning and build the story around that or have a cool story with no meaning and then find that meaning and go back and work it in. Like in *Powers*, it's a superhero universe seen through the eyes of police. The theme is how it is observed by the media and everyday man. What came first, was it the media seeing heroes, or a superhero universe seen through the eyes of cops?

be more open about how I write the script. I write a list of scenes and what each scene's point is or what the big image of the scene is—the moment—and then I let the characters go for a ride.

OEMING: In *Powers*, we tend to stay away from the big exploding ending. We are more comfortable with a character-driven or psychological ending than a Jerry Bruckheimer explosion, action through character rather than spectacle. I've always felt it was because spectacle endings are, well, not that smart. I love simple stories, like how in *Bastard Samurai*, it's a basic revenge story.

BENDIS: Boy, I really liked that plug you just tossed in like that all casual and shit. I am proud of you, you've come a long way.

OEMING: I'm not calling my own ending dumb, but where I like to chop the head off of my villain, you would tend to have the villain be defeated through character rather than physical action. Is that because you find the physical ending too simple?

BENDIS: Um, no. Basically anyone can blow up the set James Bond-style at the end. A chimp could do that. Doesn't meant it isn't satisfying, but I always look for the smarter or unexpected route.

OEMING: Are you afraid of writing an ending that doesn't engage enough thought from the reader? Zhang Yimou's movie *Hero* really struck me as having a Bendis Ending.

BENDIS: At first it was the clichés of the superhero genre through the harder eyes of the cops. And then when we both decided to add the *VH-1 Behind the Music* twist to it, that every arc has some footing in a famous rock star story, and that's when it became magic to us. That's when I knew it was worth publishing, because now it was about a lot of things.

OEMING: How do you structure a story? I think now you mull it over in your head and then go straight to writing, but was there a time when you wrote step-by-step outlines and built it around that?

BENDIS: I think I learned how to do that, so now I am much more interested in fucking around with the three act structure. Like, with you I have shorthand, so I can

BENDIS: Hmm, that's nice, I saw this Jenna Jameson movie that I thought ended a lot like one of your books. Ha!

Well, no. I mean, it's all about that particular story. I love a big action scene, but I also think a person hitting another person is a big damn deal, you know? You ever get slapped? It fucks up your whole day. So, I try to write the action with that in mind, and as endings go, I like to leave it a little vague, let the audience think about it for a second, maybe.

OEMING: What bothers you most about writers today in comics? I don't mean outside of the page, but what is the most common problem you see in their works?

BENDIS: Other than the lazy, alcoholic poseurs that are more into their image than their work, I think what really bums me out is I see a lot of comics that were failed movie pitches, or people writing comics to sell as properties. Now, we both have had the luck of selling movie properties, including *Powers*—but we never, ever, ever consciously created something for that purpose. Comics are a vital medium and form of expression and entertainment, not a stepping stone or a slum for your shit *Aliens* knock-offs. I really hate all the clutter that is thrown into *Previews* that is so clearly made to get Hollywood's attention.

OEMING: What is it specifically about the writers you admire? The work, not the person. Greg Rucka, for instance.

BENDIS: He is a real writer. He is the best technical writer I have ever met or talked to. And he isn't afraid to talk about the craft, like so many are. Many writers are afraid to talk about it because they think people will find out how full of shit they are.

OEMING: Mamet.

BENDIS: There's so much I couldn't even type it here. He is my guru. I have a huge book of interviews by him that I keep on my nightstand like the Bible, I go to it if I am lost. Seriously.

OEMING: Alan Moore.

BENDIS: He's the gold standard. He's like our DeNiro. He is so good so often that he is often taken for granted. I won two consecutive best writer Eisners, and I don't think I did anything as inventive as anything he did in one double-page spread of *Promethea*. It seems insane to me that his books aren't higher on the charts. But listen, he's a witch living in the blue dimension, so he's fine.

Okay, I got some for you. Mike Mignola.

OEMING: He's my Mamet. Honestly, when I am lost or uninspired, I flip through his work. The looseness, especially. He's not afraid of the line, he's not a slave to it, he rules it! I love tight artists, I really do, but the tight lines often suck the life out of their work. Mike's lines are so loose they can be sloppy and abstract and still work. Besides the lines, Mike's work exudes a mood I find almost hypnotic. He is mythology on the page, his work evokes the subconscious.

BENDIS: Alex Toth.

OEMING: Storytelling and black spotting. While he doesn't do storytelling like I do, I like a much more "in-between" feel to the panels, he cuts to the chase. He's the master of simplicity and yet his work is more complex than most. He's a genius and a master of the medium. His black spotting and composition is just something few, if any, can compare to. My favorite work of his is the late '60s into the early '80s. I still write him from time to time and he writes back.

BENDIS: Bruce Timm.

OEMING: He actually helped me understand Alex Toth's work better. From Timm, I learned a lot about form, keeping the exterior of a body simple, smooth lines on the outside that make the character flow, not interrupted by lines that break the form. Timm flows better than any artist I know of.

BENDIS: Adam Hughes.

OEMING: Adam taught me a lot. Hands on. I worked with him when we lived in the same town. We met just before he broke into comics. He introduced me to Steve Rude's work (Neil Vokes showed him Rude, Neil showed me Toth and Timm, Neil is another big influence on me) and taught me a lot about storytelling. There is a panel in a *Star Trek* novel he did where there are guys running off a ship in line. He drew them as if it were animation, each guy in the next pose a person would be in, as if running, left foot, right foot, and in-betweens. We talked a lot about art and artists. He tends to like more refined artists while I like them looser and sloppy. Adam is also a very close friend.

BENDIS: Steranko.

OEMING: I've never been into Steranko's work. If you see any there, it's the Jack Kirby influence probably, or the influences of others. I love Jim's work, but didn't discover it until recently.

BENDIS: David Mack. In fact, let's gossip about all the shit we know about David Mack.

OEMING: I happen to know that David is a great wrestler and can fart really loud. Thankfully, he never farted on me when we wrestled. His design sense, the lack of respect for the borders of a page, really influenced me! You can see that a lot in *Bulletproof Monk* and in the *Oni Press Color Special* issue with the *Powers* story we goofed around on. All done in love. He's also in need of Ritalin.

What is something you see in your favorite writers (not one I mentioned above) that you like the least?

BENDIS: Well, I think I get annoyed at how criticized they are by people who don't get it. I get very annoyed at how much shit Aaron Sorkin gets from critics when his work is so vastly superior to everything else on television, it's amazing to me.

You hate *The Watchmen*? Explain this travesty.

OEMING: I don't hate it, it just doesn't get me. I think it's because it's been so influential on other books that when I try reading it, all those lessons have been used in good and bad ways so the effect is watered down when I read the original. I've tried reading it three times, and not once does it interest me. Now don't get me wrong, I love Alan Moore. I even love his music. In fact, there are ways I like his music more than the writing. I love most of his work. *Parliament of Justice* is very influenced by *V For Vendetta*. I just don't "get" *Watchmen*. It's just a mental shortcoming on my part. I'd die to work with Moore.

BENDIS: For a life-long comic professional, you don't seem very into comics on a monthly basis. Do you read a lot of comics? What do you read, what's your favorite comic? Why are you so standoffish to the business on some levels?

OEMING: It's odd, but it's like this with a lot of comics people I know. The more you make comics, the less you read them. Nothing makes me more happy than writing or drawing comics, but reading them doesn't hold my interest. In fact, I rarely read the finished product of my own book. I think the last issue of *Powers* I read when it was done is like issue #7. No shit. Same with *Hammer*. But with *Bastard*, I did read those when it was done to measure if we went too far in not explaining everything or *Parliament* because it was

Neil and I, and that was a goal to meet. But for the most part I don't read my own comics, I enjoy making them, not reading them.

I've been reading the *Daredevil* trades and I fucking love those. I've read Rucka's *Whiteout* recently. Other than *Hellboy*, I don't read monthly comics. I also stay away from the business in general, who's doing what, what new books are out, who is running what company. I feel that if it's not my business, I'm not going to waste my energy on it. All my energy goes into my work and family. There's a war between Marvel and DC these days and I couldn't be less interested. Also, I just don't understand a lot of it, I'm not business minded.

Don't get me wrong, I love comics, but I love making them more than anything else. It's like that a lot in life for me, I'm about the journey, not the destination.

What do you see in, say, a Scorsese film that repeats itself as a flaw in storytelling? I know the aforementioned Robert McKee hates *Goodfellas*, but he didn't elaborate, he simply laughed at it. What do you think it was?

BENDIS: Sour grapes. *Goodfellas* didn't hold to his predetermined structure values and it worked. So he shits on it. Though I wholeheartedly recommend his book. I am not a slave to it, bitchy is bitchy, cranking on *Goodfellas* is bitchy.

OEMING: When you read a story or watch a movie, and you are trying to analyze it, what are the things you are looking for?

BENDIS: Why it works or why it doesn't. I am mostly examining how scenes work juxtaposed against each other. There's where the magic is. How about you?

OEMING: Mostly it's visuals, but in stories, I look for truth. It can be a super wacky film, but it has to have its own truth. I just saw *Kill Bill* and there are ridiculous things going on but for this film, it's all true and works. I'm still learning to learn.

What's one of the newest things you've learned about writing? Where did you learn it from? Watching a film, reading a book?

BENDIS: Well, I am very interested in breaking out of my comfort zone, there are things I know I do well, and there are things I do not know if I do well, so I am trying to do them to experience it and see if it works. In *Powers*, particularly, I have attempted styles and genres I never thought I would try, specifically to see why.

What's the one thing about your art that you think you need to improve and why? And why haven't you tried it yet? And what are you waiting for?

OEMING: Hah, taking my time! I'd really love to have a project where I can slow down and think the shit out of each page and the story as a whole. Right now, it's largely instinct built from years of hands-on work, but I'd like to approach a project with no time restraints and really work it. I'd also like to work on my backgrounds more. I think taking my time would help, but I'm a speed freak.

In *Powers*, we have total freedom to do whatever we want or what the story wants us to do. At Marvel, you don't have that freedom. You have editors and bosses and characters that have to maintain a continuity. I've found that what you've done with *Daredevil* is amazing, you actually found room for character growth there, something rare and hard to do in a mainstream, established series. How much does that hold you back? Especially on *Ultimate Spider-Man*, I imagine there's much less you can do. Shouldn't Mary Jane be smoking pot and having sex with Peter?

BENDIS: Who says she doesn't? Well, I don't see the limitations at Marvel as limitations. I see them as opportunities to be creative. I read this interview with Ridley Scott recently and he said nothing makes him more inspired than a budget, he said every limitation put before him has created a situation where he forced himself to be more creative than he would have been otherwise. I have the same feeling. Also, it's the juxtaposition of creator-owned and work-for-hire that has made my work so fulfilling to me. Both experiences have pros and cons and I find they feed off each other, I think it has a lot to do with the way a lot of people have responded to my work.

Also, Marvel is pretty damn trusting of me and I have been allowed to go out on the plank many a time. Anal anyone? And I will forever be the guy who used the F-word in a Marvel comic first. See, you have had some unfulfilling work-for-hire experiences, you need a fulfilling one, and I am going to make you do one so you can experience how awesome it could be.

OEMING: *Great!* I can't wait. Maybe that's the one I can take my time on. Obviously drawing an issue of a comic takes longer than writing an issue of a comic--or at least it should. *Powers* is my love but also a monthly gig, which can be hard at times, grinding work.

BENDIS: Boo-hoo, wahh-wahh.

OEMING: I do my "side projects" really to keep me sane. Even though you write several books at a time, how do you keep any of those gigs from becoming stale?

BENDIS: If they got stale, I would bail in two seconds, life is too short. And it's my name on the cover. Also, I stay ahead of schedule, so sometimes I don't write, let's say, *Powers* for months at a time, and then write it constantly for weeks. I write it when I am inspired to. That's the real key o everything. You have the attention span of a ferret full of Snickers bars, so it's harder for you to focus, but you're also a martial arts master, so it's odd. You are a conundrum wrapped in a package of contradiction.

DEMING: Thanks! How much longer do you see *Powers* going?

BENDIS: It's over. Bye, Mike.

DEMING: We know the ending, and we've talked it over. Not in terms of issues or years, but how many story lines do you see coming up? We've promised to never write or draw *Powers* beyond the amount of fresh ideas we have.

BENDIS: Exactly, we'll know when it's time to wrap it up. I think both of us were surprised at how challenging this year was creatively, we really pushed each other. I don't feel like we're even near the end.

DEMING: We've done less police procedurals, which are my favorite stories.

BENDIS: Me, too. They're fun to write. Why are you so into them?

DEMING: The pacing. I have trouble mixing noir and heroes. Sometimes you have Pete darken and thicken the lines because I have that problem. When I see cops walk into a room with a dead superhero, however, it's all mood and shadows. People are in danger in the *Powers* universe, you never know when Deena, Walker, the Captain, whomever might get killed. I like the dirtiness of the work.

They do unfortunately have repeating conventions to the story that people think are tired or predictable. Like there must be a murder in a murder investigation, there must be a body, it must be a hero, etc. How do we continue to do those in such a way that our less astute readers won't perceive it as repetitious? *Homicide* and *Law and Order* do it every week.

BENDIS: Also, at this point, there are tons of *Powers* knock-offs. I know I sound like Howard Stern, but man, I look through *Previews* and I get a nosebleed. It's flattering and I welcome it, but a lot of these publishers fucking rejected *Powers*, so it's funny. But I think we have the freedom and the vision to stay ahead of the pack, so that's not that much of a concern. I think that we certainly shocked people with the last couple of stories, I think most people know for certain that even if the story starts with a body, they don't know how it's going to end. But yeah, it's my favorite part, too. We'll get back to it very soon.

But you just like drawing the talking heads.

DEMING: How much do you listen to your detractors? I know we get tons of mail saying how great we are, but it's always the few that tell us we suck that bug us, or even worse, the shrug-off. At what point do we take

that into account? If we continually laugh it off, we can become one of the many burned out creators who only listen to the cheers who think they are still doing great work when it's actually crap.

BENDIS: That's a very good question. I don't know if I have an answer yet, because there's also the fact that it is absolutely impossible to make everyone happy. Every book I have ever been involved with has been someone's favorite and someone's least favorite, one person cried, the other person was bored, I don't know what the answer is. But a lot of times the critic tells you where he is coming from, which qualifies the critique. In the review he will say, "I wish *Powers* was more photo realistic." And we have to look at that and say, "Well, it's not, so what's your point?" That's like saying, "I wish *The Matrix* was funnier." They weren't trying to be funny, so why even analyze it like that? Or a critic will say, "I have been reading comics for fifty-five years and Stan Lee could have told that story in six pages." Like somehow I don't know I am taking a different approach to the scenes than they did in the '60s, like somehow that idea totally eludes me. So, I don't know. Our approval rating is pretty high and people do vote with their wallets, so I guess that's really what you have to listen to. But even then, how much do you give people what they think they want versus what you need to say as a storyteller? See? No easy answer, I do not know. I think the best thing we both have done is not spend our time online arguing with people that disagree with us aesthetically. We let the work speak for itself. A lot of our peers bury themselves with online arguments when they should be working on the book. What it does do for me is it makes me work harder, because I know there's no bullshit that will fly, the people speak out. You know? But I know that sometimes my critics annoy you a lot, more than they do me. Also, people don't even get when they are reacting exactly how we want them to, like with a tease or a cliffhanger, some people get so fucking angry about a cliffhanger and they don't even see how much fun they are having. I'm like, "See, you care. It's fun."

I know in your porn chatrooms, you get a lot of criticism for your flowery metaphors, how do you deal with it?

OEMING: I deal with it in a big, pink bunny suit...Anyway, often in *Powers* I'm running against deadlines and can take shortcuts, such as not doing a full background or keeping the camera too close too often to avoid drawing more. Aside from that, what do you think I have to work on the most in my work?

BENDIS: I think you need to be more photo realistic. My only concern with you has always been style consistency, you have so many things you can do and so many tools at your disposal that you often forget the power of a consistent line through a story arc. We talk about that a lot. But this is a problem of you being too talented and eating too much sugar more than anything else.

OEMING: That's true, I especially think you see that in this compilation. As of *Foreverman*, however, I've decided to stay with the brush. I think I got the pen out of my *Powers* system. What about yourself? what is your biggest weakness? I don't mean the stuff you stay away from writing, like fantasy or group books, but in the work that you do, what is your weakest ability?

BENDIS: Clearly I have trouble with the format of a comic. I have trouble keeping to my page count and have for years. I either go over my page count or take a scene that could be a nice four pager and I cram it into two pages because I have no wiggle room. It bothers me. Also, I can't spell almost to the point of retardation, and like when I won all those nice awards this summer, I felt like a fake or something. Why don't I know the difference between "their" and "they're"? I mean, I know the difference, but I don't do it.

OEMING: If I had to name one weakness in your work, I'd have to say it was your inability to self-edit. I'm sure you see how much you actually cut out, but sometimes I look at the amount of words on a page and it goes beyond a wordy page to an impossibly wordy page. Sometimes I can't understand why there are so many words on a page. Sometimes there's as many words as there is art. Why can't you look at a page and say, "I have to cut this way down"? I'm not complaining, hey, it's less for me to fucking draw! But on a scale of 1-10, sometimes you're on a 12 or 13 when it comes to a page with too much dialogue.

BENDIS: See, that was a very wordy response, Mr. Blah Blah Blah! I agree in theory, and often I think you are surprised by what I yank off the page at the last minute.

OEMING: Wait a minute, you "yank off" on the page? No, that doesn't surprise me...anyway, I know comics are limited in space, but instead of cramming lots of words into one place, why not change the pacing of the story so you end an issue on a different climax in order to pan out those dialogue scenes to make them fit without overcrowding the page? Just move the events down and find new climaxes if there's not enough room that issue?

BENDIS: See, I know I just gave you a bitch of a script this week and you are reeling, but, honestly, I fall in love with a particular cliffhanger, or a decide that this amount of story is worth the $2.95 we have to charge. I hate that comics are so expensive, so I try to cram a lot in. I feel very beholden to people to give them a good read.

But if I didn't write all those balloons, you'd have to draw backgrounds, so why are you pulling at this string?

OEMING: Hey, you said we had to ask the hard questions! Other than asking mean ones, like why you eat so much candy, I'm asking professional ones like this.

A major shift has happened in comics, where the art was more important than the story, to the point we had no stories. Erik Larsen even announced that writers were no longer needed! Now the shift has gone, thankfully, to the writers, but do you think in mainstream comics that's gone too far? Sometimes people just want to see shit blow up and men fight men. By sometimes I mean once an issue.

BENDIS: And, honestly, ninety percent of comics still do that. Only a few are allowed the arrogance/luxury to do whatever they want storywise. It just, to my shock above all others, there is a big audience for story driven-comics and most can wait for the fight scene, they don't need it.

OEMING: I know you're big into politics, but I never see it in your work, why is that? And please, don't change, I hate that whole world and those who drag it into their writing.

BENDIS: Oh, my politics, or I should say my feelings about politics, are all over my books. When you say politics, people think that means I'm like Susan Sarandon and I'm protesting and shit. No, I am aware and obsessed with the murky water that is our political process and how our government works. And more importantly how it affects us on a day-to-day basis, and *that* is all over my work. All my characters are oppressed by the man, as they are by your puritanical view of women.

OEMING: We love people talking about *Powers*, about the character stuff. At what point should we spell things out for people? Maybe long after we're done? People keep asking me if Deena killed Johnny Stomps, and I just ask them what they think. They also ask me why if Walker suspects she did it, why he doesn't really do anything about it.

BENDIS: As far as I can tell, most people get it, and then there's all the fun everyone has talking about it online. I say we let them have the fun. Why are you trying to spoil their fun, Mike? Fun-spoiling Nazi!

OEMING: I love when you write a character as an asshole and then we learn they are more valiant than most of the characters in that same world. *Powers* characters have a real depth. Do you find that in real life very often?

BENDIS: Yes and no, often I hope that this asshole I am talking to has some depth only to find out that they don't. I guess that is what art is for, so we can have what we want in life.

OEMING: While it's not your thing, do you think you will ever want to write a sci-fi story or fantasy-based story? You have been branching out more into group books, which you swore off once...I think you could write a really intelligent sci-fi or fantasy book, something much needed in that genre and a challenge that I think would bring out new dimensions in your work.

BENDIS: Well, technically all Marvel comics are sci-fi comics. I mean, they all have that sci-fi element. I'm writing *Ultimate Fantastic Four* and that's about as sci-fi as it gets. You probably can't tell because of *all the talking*.

OEMING: Looking over the issues of *Powers*, what would you have done differently in any given issue? Dig deep, find something.

BENDIS: Well, if we felt we told the perfect *Powers* story, we wouldn't have to keep doing them. How about you?

OEMING: Just art stuff. Walker isn't consistent physically in the first four issues, the linework changing mid-story in *Anarchy*, not pulling the camera back often enough. When I look at my art, I just look for the bad things, my eye is drawn right to it.

What about your main-stream work? Is there anything you wish you had written or addressed differently given hindsight? Something you look back on and say, "Shit, I missed this aspect of the story, or didn't emphasize enough of such and such."

BENDIS: If I did *Elektra* again I would just go all hot chick kung-fu and not try to be all brainy with it. I like the story we told, but if I did it again, I would save that story for another time and just deliver the ass-kicking Elektra I and everyone else wanted.

Also, *Daredevil: Ninja* was a textbook example of the artist and writer having no ability to communicate with each other. Marvel offered me a parachute and I didn't take it, I should have taken it. I felt I could save it, but I couldn't. There's good stuff in there, but it could have been great. Thank God for Alex Maleev.

you seem to think you're the grunt artist of *Judge Dredd*. So, my question is, do you ever think you'll take a second and step outside yourself and look around and go, "Oh, hey, ok, I made it"? I'm not saying be an asshole rock star fuckhead, because I hate that too, but many times I wish you knew your place in the biz.

OEMING: Yeah, that was a good example of communication breakdown. Another great Zeppelin song...

BENDIS: You got a pretty sordid comics past, Mr. *Edward Penis-hands*, how about you?

OEMING: Actually I don't have any problems with those early porn books, they were goofy. But everything up till *Powers*, with the exception of *Bulletproof Monk*, parts of *Ship of Fools* and *Foot Soldiers*, hurts my eyes to look at. I wish I had just gotten a real job and let my art grow out of the public eye!

What are the top five questions you hate being asked the most in interviews? We get a lot of repeat questions to the point it seems like the interviewer has put no thought into it.

BENDIS: Well, listen, being asked a question over and over is better than not being asked anything by anyone. Speaking of which, I both admire and am annoyed by how much you don't know you're a big deal in comics. You are one of the best artists in comics, you have won awards, all of your projects are successful, you have sold all kinds of stuff, yet

OEMING: I know I've "made it," but honestly, you can take the boy out of the ghetto, but not the ghetto out of the boy. I come from a really mentally beat-down background and will always carry something about me that says I haven't done enough. Remember I said I love the journey, not the destination? I think the bad part of that is I always feel like I'm on the journey and once I reach the destination, I'm dissatisfied and want to move on. I'm amazed I have just enough common sense to not self-destruct. Maybe because I've seen enough of that in those I love. *Powers* keeps changing and evolving so it always feels like a journey. Thanks for the confidence, I've always been grateful to you for that. That's why you're the only one allowed to call me a Nazi.

BENDIS: What do you want from *Powers* next year creatively?

OEMING: I'd like to see Walker and Deena become more personable to each other, eventhough I like their standoffish relationship. They really are opposite sides of the same coin at this point. I like how they react to each other, it's unpredictable. Deena is unpredictable. After *Foreverman*, I really look forward to getting back to those two. I love how you write them. A gunfight would be cool, too, one where someone shoots a gas tank and it explodes at the end. :)

— PERFECT SHOT

WALKER FRONT | AVON 12·31·01

WALKER
STATUE DESIGNS

RIGHT/BACK

BACK/AVA 1-1-02

PERFECT
SHOT

L'EFFRANT

HEADS TOO BIG

PERFECT

RIGHT/FRONT/Ara 1-1-02